The Iliad

Homer

STUDENT PACKET

NOTE:

The trade book edition of the novel used to prepare this guide is found in the Novel Units catalog and on the Novel Units website. Using other editions may have varied page references.

Please note: We have assigned Interest Levels based on our knowledge of the themes and ideas of the books included in the Novel Units sets, however, please assess the appropriateness of this novel or trade book for the age level and maturity of your students prior to reading with them. You know your students best!

ISBN 978-1-56137-753-4

Copyright infringement is a violation of Federal Law.

© 2020 by Novel Units, Inc., St. Louis, MO. All rights reserved. No part of this publication may be reproduced, translated, stored in a retrieval system, or transmitted in any way or by any means (electronic, mechanical, photocopying, recording, or otherwise) without prior written permission from Novel Units, Inc.

Reproduction of any part of this publication for an entire school or for a school system, by for-profit institutions and tutoring centers, or for commercial sale is strictly prohibited.

Novel Units is a registered trademark of Conn Education.

Printed in the United States of America.

To order, contact your local school supply store, or:

Toll-Free Fax: 877.716.7272
Phone: 888.650.4224
3901 Union Blvd., Suite 155
St. Louis, MO 63115

sales@novelunits.com

novelunits.com

Name_____

The Iliad
Activity #1: Anticipation Guide
Use Before Reading

Directions: With a partner, rate and discuss the following statements on a scale of 1-6. Keep these ratings in mind as you read the *Iliad* and consider whether Homer and various characters in his poem feel the same way you do.

```
1-----------2-----------3-----------4-----------5-----------6
agree                                                disagree
strongly                                             strongly
```

_____ 1. Revenge is the best medicine.

_____ 2. Winning isn't everything; it's how you play the game that counts.

_____ 3. Hell hath no fury like a woman scorned.

_____ 4. All's fair in love and war.

_____ 5. A friend in need is a friend indeed.

_____ 6. The ends justify the means.

_____ 7. It is important to "save face" at any cost.

_____ 8. It all comes around; you will get what you deserve in the end.

_____ 9. You should take care of yourself first, then worry about saving the world.

_____ 10. You should be willing to die for your country.

_____ 11. Life is hard.

_____ 12. Real men don't eat quiche.

_____ 13. If mothers and wives were in charge, there would be no war.

_____ 14. Most wars are fought for material gain.

_____ 15. Most wars are a battle of good against evil.

_____ 16. You should express your anger.

_____ 17. It's not healthy to walk around with a chip on your shoulder.

_____ 18. I'd rather be a live coward than a dead hero.

_____ 19. Only the good die young.

© Novel Units, Inc.   All rights reserved

Name_____

The Iliad
Activity #2: Vocabulary
Use During Reading

Robert Fitzgerald has translated the *Iliad* from Greek to English. Even in the translation there are plenty of words that may be unfamiliar to you.

Directions:
(a) Predict whether each of the following words refers to a fighting maneuver (M), a body part (B), a piece of armor or weaponry (W), a positive trait (+), a negative trait (–).
(b) Brainstorm possible definitions. Write down one or two synonyms.
(c) Use each word in a sentence. Have fun writing imaginative sentences—and then comparing your efforts with Homer's. (The numbers after each word refer to the Book and line number where you will find the word: 1, 344 = Book 1, line 344.)

1. poltroon (1, 344)
   a) ___ ; b) _____ , _____
   c) _____

2. siege (2, 431)
   a) ___ ; b) _____ , _____
   c) _____

3. sortie (2, 968)
   a) ___ ; b) _____ , _____
   c) _____

4. routed (5, 795)
   a) ___ ; b) _____ , _____
   c) _____

5. virile (6, 220)
   a) ___ ; b) _____ , _____
   c) _____

6. nape (7, 13)
   a) ___ ; b) _____ , _____
   c) _____

7. craven (9, 49)
   a) ___ ; b) _____ , _____
   c) _____

8. entrails (10, 11)
   a) ___ ; b) _____ , _____
   c) _____

© Novel Units, Inc.   All rights reserved

Name_____

The Iliad
Study Questions
Use During Reading

Study Questions

Book One

1. In the first lines, what does Homer ask the Muse to do?
2. What started the quarrel between Akhilleus and Agamémnon? How did the god Apollo make the Greek army suffer—and why?
3. What did Agamémnon take from Akhilleus after he let Khrysêis go?
4. Why did Akhilleus come to fight the Trojans—and why did he refuse to fight them any more?
5. What appeal did Thetis make to Zeus?
6. Why did Zeus threaten to "lay [his] inexorable hands upon" his consort, Hêra? (line 653)

Book Two

1. Briefly describe the dream that Zeus made Agamémnon have.
2. What did Agamémnon do as a result of his dream?
3. Why did Nestor suggest that the soldiers should be organized by nation and clan?

Book Three

1. What were the terms of the contest between Paris and Menelâos? (What would happen if Paris were victorious? If he lost?)
2. How did Aphrodítê protect Paris during the contest with Menelâos?
3. Cite one or two lines from this book that show Helen's scorn for Paris.
4. Why did the Greeks claim victory after the contest between Paris and Menelâos?

Book Four

1. How did Zeus's suggestion about the outcome of the contest between Menelâos and Paris anger Hêra?
2. How did Athêna trick Pándaros?
3. What was the result of Menelâos's injury?

© Novel Units, Inc.   All rights reserved

Book Five
1. Who killed Pándaros?
2. Name two gods and/or goddesses who sided with the Greeks.
3. Name three gods and/or goddesses who sided with the Trojans.
4. Name two gods who returned to Olympus after being wounded in the battle.

Book Six
1. Whose brother was Hektor?
2. Why did Hektor tell the Trojan women to make offerings to Athêna?
3. Why did Diomêdês and Glaukos decide not to fight each other?
4. Who "began to wail, terrified by his father's great war helm"? (lines 543-44)

Book Seven
1. What was the outcome of the duel between Hektor and Aías?
2. Why was a truce called?
3. Cite a line that supports the idea that at least some of the Trojans wanted Paris to give Helen up to the Greeks.
4. What offer by the Trojans did the Greeks refuse?

Book Eight
1. What command did Zeus give the gods and goddesses?
2. Who led the Trojans in driving the Greeks back to their encampment?
3. According to Zeus's prediction, when would Akhilleus rejoin the fighting?
4. Cite a line or two that describe where the Trojans spend the night.

Book Nine
1. Who stood up to disagree when Agamémnon called for retreat?
2. Who were the three emissaries?
3. On what mission did Lord Nestor send the emissaries?
4. How did the emissaries fail in their mission?

Name_____

The Iliad
Study Questions
page 3

Book Ten

1. What challenge did Nestor make—and Diomêdês accept?
2. Why did Diomêdês choose Odysseus to accompany him?
3. How did Diomêdês and Odysseus trick Dolôn?
4. How did Diomêdês and Odysseus end up on Trojan horses?

Book Eleven

1. List four Greek heroes who were injured in the attack.
2. What message did Zeus send with Iris?
3. Why did Akhilleus send Patróklos to Nestor?
4. What advice did Nestor suggest Patróklos give Akhilleus?
5. How did Patróklos help Eurypylos?

Book Twelve

1. Who led the Trojan soldiers in their attack on the Greek fortifications?
2. Describe one piece of advice by Poulydamas that Hektor accepted.
3. Describe one piece of advice by Poulydamas that Hektor rejected.
4. What brave Trojan charged the Greek wall with his cousin, Glaukos?

Book Thirteen

1. What "Earthshaker" defied Zeus to aid the Greeks?
2. Around what two fiery warriors did the Greeks make a stand?
3. How did Paris respond when his brother called him a "bad-luck charm"? (line 884)
4. To which side did Zeus plan to give victory?

Book Fourteen

1. Name three Greek heroes who were wounded.
2. What did Odysseus think of Agamémnon's plan to launch the ships?
3. How did Hêra defy Zeus and help the Greeks?
4. Why did Hektor leave the fighting field?

© Novel Units, Inc.   All rights reserved

Name_____

The Iliad
Study Questions
page 4

Book Fifteen
1. What message did Zeus send Poseidon via Iris?
2. Summarize Zeus's prediction about Patróklos, Hektor, Akhilleus, and the taking of Troy.
3. What god led the Trojans as they advanced on the Greek ships?
4. Why did Patróklos return to Akhilleus?

Book Sixteen
1. What did Patróklos persuade Akhilleus to let him do?
2. What did Akhilleus lend Patróklos?
3. Who killed Patróklos?
4. What did Patróklos predict, with his final breath?

Book Seventeen
1. What did Hektor take from Patróklos's body?
2. What did Glaukos want to do with Patróklos's body?
3. Why did Hektor fight for Patróklos's body? Did he end up with it?
4. Why was a runner sent to Akhilleus?

Book Eighteen
1. Why was Antílokhos afraid that Akhilleus might slash his own throat?
2. Whose death did Thetis predict?
3. What did Akhilleus vow to do before Patróklos's funeral?
4. Why did Thetis go to Hêphaistos?

Book Nineteen
1. Describe Thetis's promise and advice to her son.
2. After Akhilleus reconciled with Agamémnon, what did Odysseus advise Akhilleus to do for his men?
3. Describe the gifts Agamémnon gave Akhilleus—and the promise Agamémnon made about Brisêis.
4. How did the words of the horse, Xánthos, anger Akhilleus?

© Novel Units, Inc.   All rights reserved

Name

Book Twenty
1. Name the gods who sided with the Greeks and those who supported the Trojans.
2. Why did Poseidon help Aineías escape?
3. Which god helped protect Hektor—and how?
4. Did Akhilleus show Trôs mercy?

Book Twenty-One
1. Why was the god of the river Xánthos angry with Akhilleus?
2. What gods fought against what other individual gods?
3. How did Apollo protect the Trojan, Agênor?
4. Why did Apollo assume Agênor's identity?

Book Twenty-Two
1. Why did Hektor remain outside the gates when other Trojans took cover inside?
2. How did Hektor's parents plead with him—and what was their effect on him?
3. How did Athêna trick Hektor into fighting Akhilleus?
4. What did Akhilleus do after killing Hektor?

Book Twenty-Three
1. What did Patróklos's ghost request Akhilleus to do?
2. What preparations did Akhilleus make before Patróklos's body was burned on the funeral pyre?
3. What did Akhilleus do with Patróklos's bones?
4. What are some of the funeral games Akhilleus presided over—and some of the prizes he supplied?

Book Twenty-Four
1. Why did Zeus send Iris to Thetis and to Priam?
2. What did Thetis tell her son to do—and how did he react?
3. How was Priam's reaction to the idea of retrieving Hektor's body different from his wife's?
4. How does the *Iliad* end?

Name_____

The Iliad
Activity #3: Your Mythology IQ
Use Before Reading

Your Mythology IQ

From the myths and fairy tales you have read, the stories you've heard, and the cartoons you've watched, you have probably picked up a lot of information about Greek gods and goddesses.

Numerous gods and goddesses make an appearance in the *Iliad*. Some of these didn't acquire the reputation you may know about until people after Homer told stories about them. (For instance, Achilles [Akhilleus in this translation] didn't have his problematic heel in the *Iliad*.)

Match each of the names on the left with the description you think fits best.

___ 1. Zeus   a. god of war
___ 2. Hêra   b. supreme god of the Greeks
___ 3. Apollo   c. god of fire
___ 4. Poseidon   d. god of music and prophecy
___ 5. Arês   e. queen of Heaven; goddess of marriage
___ 6. Aphrodíte   f. goddess of the moon, hunting, fertility
___ 7. Artemis   g. god of sea and earthquakes
___ 8. Hermês   h. goddess of wisdom
___ 9. Athêna   i. goddess of love and beauty
___ 10. Hêphaistos   j. messenger of the gods

Your Mythology IQ

Scoring:
9–10	Holy cow! You know your gods and goddesses.
6–9	Your standing on Mt. Olympus is a little shaky.
less than 6	You are about to make a lot of new acquaintances in high places.

Name_____

The Iliad
Activity #4: Character Relationships
Use After Reading Book One

Directions: You can use graphics (charts and drawings) to help you remember "who's who" in the *Iliad*. Below is a list of some important characters in Book One of the *Iliad*:

Akhilleus	Agamémnon	Khryséis	Apollo
Meneláos	Paris	Aphrodítê	Briseis
Zeus	Hêra		

As you read the poem (and/or as other groups present books of the poem to the class) fill in and extend the following graphic. Draw a symbol in each box to represent the character—e.g., a lightning bolt for Zeus. Write each character's name in the appropriate blank.

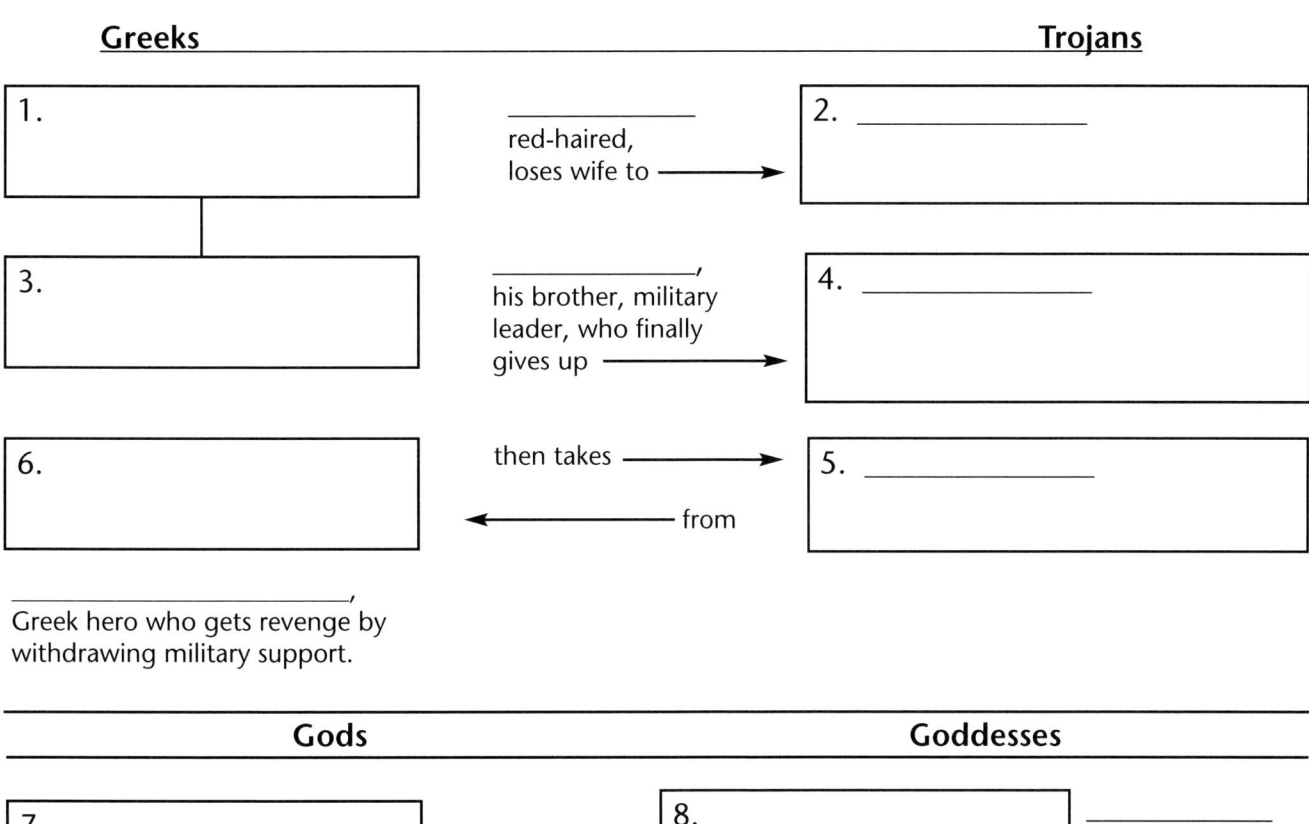

_____,
Greek hero who gets revenge by withdrawing military support.

Name

The Iliad
Activity #5: Critical Thinking/Creative Writing
Use After Reading Book Fifteen

Directions: You are Patróklos. You decide to write to a newspaper columnist about your friend, Akhilleus.

Step 1: On separate paper, finish the letter begun for you, below:

Dear Gabby:
My problem is with my best friend, Akhilleus. He often looks to me for advice, and this time the stakes are so high that I want to say the right thing. It all started when he lost a woman he really cared about…

Signed,
_____

Step 2: In a small group, brainstorm possible advice Patróklos might give to Akhilleus to help him get over his anger at Agamémnon. Weigh the pros and cons of each. (A chart for organizing your ideas is shown below.) Then write a letter of advice to Patróklos, using details from the completed chart.

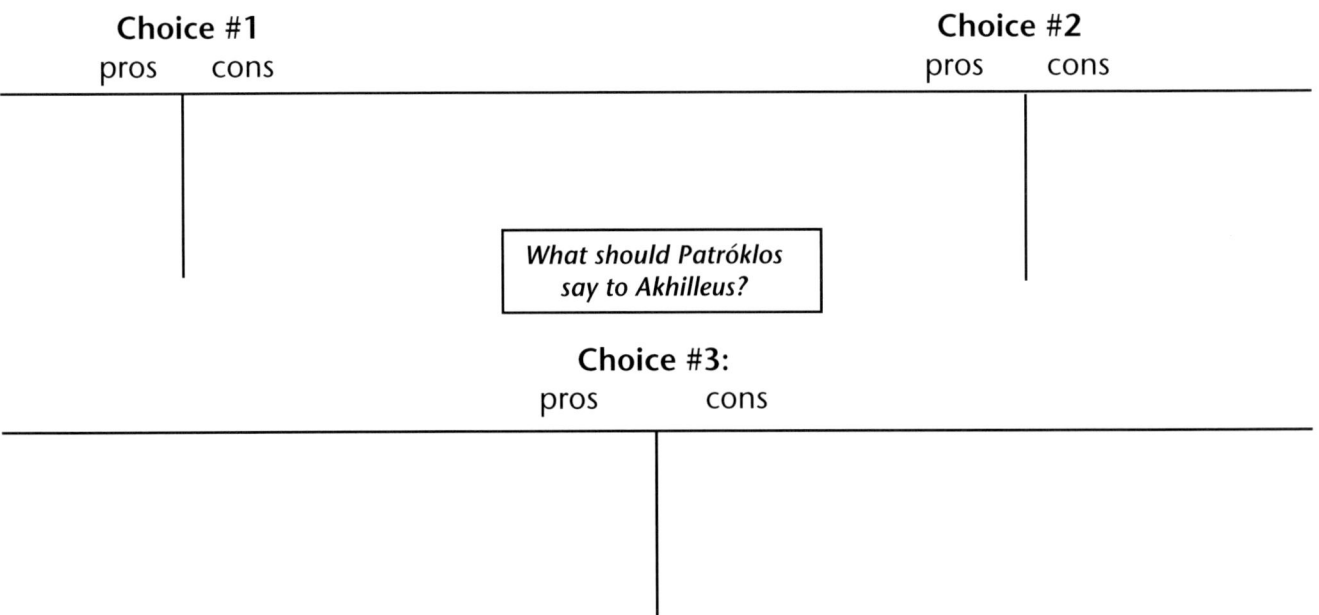

Step 3: Using details from the chart, write Gabby's letter of response.

© Novel Units, Inc. All rights reserved

Name_____

The Iliad
Activity #6: Character Sketch
Use After Reading

Directions: A **character sketch** is a brief, vivid description of a person. It includes physical characteristics—appearance, surroundings—and personality. Write a character sketch of Helen (or Akhilleus, or another character of your choice from the *Iliad*). The finished sketch should bring that character to life for the reader.

Prewriting: Imagine what Helen looks like, and get together in a small group to brainstorm a list of characteristics. Then decide which of the details will help you, the writer, convey a single, strong impression of what Helen is like. Circle these.
- What does she look like? How would you describe her eyes? her face? her hair? Is she tall? short? What are her hands and feet like? Does she have any distinguishing marks? What does her usual facial expression tell you about her personality?
- How would you describe her posture? the way she moves?
- What is her voice like? How does she speak? What is her usual tone of voice—when speaking to Paris? to Priam? to Meneláos?
- How is she dressed? What does her clothing tell you about her personality?
- What other details about Helen spring to mind? What responsibilities does she have? What does she like to do with her free time? What are her dreams and fears? How does she feel about herself?
- How do you imagine Helen's family and background? What was her relationship with Meneláos' brother like when they were children? How does she feel about him now?
- What words describe Helen? What does she value? How does she feel about life?

Writing: Choose one of the following ways to give the reader a single, focused impression of Helen (approximately 250 words):
   a. Pretend that you are someone who knows Helen well, such as Priam or Meneláos. Someone who doesn't know Helen has asked for your impression of her. Briefly tell what she is like, supporting your impression with details about her appearance, personality, and behavior.
   b. Write a short story about Helen. The story might focus on an incident before she was taken by Paris to Troy, her first few days there, the days toward the end of the war. The story should show how Helen copes with a particular problem. Remember, the reader should come away from your story with a condensed impression of what Helen is like.

Postwriting:
1. Read the character sketch aloud to your editing group. Make sure that it "sounds right." Is there a variety of long and short sentences? Do the words "flow" as you read the sketch aloud? Have you avoided unintentional repetition of words and phrases?
2. Ask for suggestions about how to make the sequence of events more clear or how to give the reader a sharper picture of Helen.
3. Revise your draft, incorporating some of these suggestions. Proofread your finished piece.

Name_____

The Iliad
Activity #7: Reader Response: Monologue
Use After Reading

Directions: Your project is to create a pair of interior monologues that reveal two characters' views of Hektor. Assume that your audience is composed of a group of high school students assigned the *Iliad*.

Prewriting:
1. Choose one of these pairs: Akhilleus and Hektor's wife Andromakhe; Priam and his wife; Aías and Paris; Poseidon and Zeus.
2. Students who have selected the same pairs discuss the characters' relationships with Hektor, then improvise conversations about Hektor.
3. After the improvisations, students discuss ad-libbed lines that seemed particularly appropriate to the character, effective, insightful. Group members suggest additional comments characters might have made.

During Writing:
As you write your interior monologues, keep these questions in mind—
1. **Voice:** What am I like? How do I sound? What tone do I use? What sort of language do I use? What is my attitude toward my subject—Hektor?
2. **Audience:** Who is the reader? What help does the reader need to understand my thoughts?
3. **Purpose:** Why am I thinking about Hektor? How will I let the audience know the situation in which I am having these thoughts about Hektor? Am I arguing with myself about something? Am I trying to make a decision? to soothe myself? to enjoy my thoughts? to figure something out about myself or Hektor?
4. **Content:** Think about these questions—What is my relationship to Hektor? How did I meet him? How does he feel about me? How do I feel about him? What do I like about him? What don't I like? Does anything about him puzzle me? What values do we share? What differences do we have?
5. **Organization:** Which type of pattern should I use to organize my ideas—chronological? spatial? order of importance? comparison? a combination? Am I a clear, logical thinker, or do my thoughts ramble? Do I have flashbacks? Do I ask myself questions? Do I hold conversations in my head? Do I joke with myself? Do I berate myself?

After Writing:
Read (or submit for reading) your interior monologues to fellow students (who have selected other pairs of characters for their monologues).

Name_____

The Iliad
Activity #8: Character Relationships
Use After Reading

Directions:

A. In a small group, talk about the relationships between the characters below. Label each arrow with a brief description of the relationship.

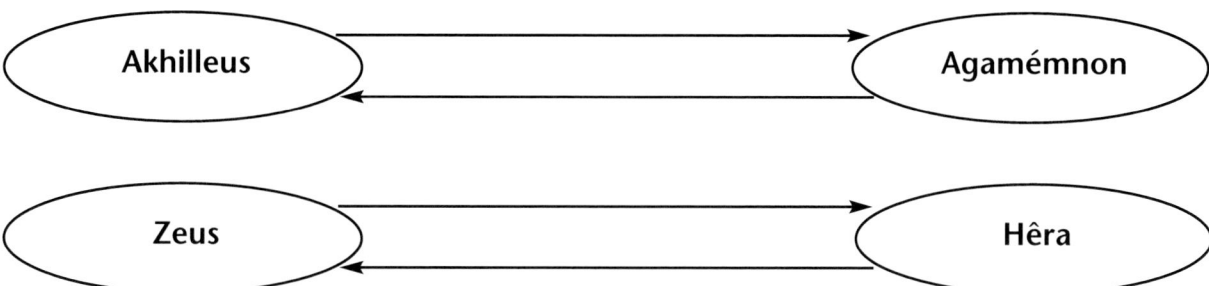

Next, write an essay analyzing one of the relationships you have discussed. How do the two get along? What is the history of their relationship? What contributes to tensions between these two—jealousy? revenge? pride? Does the nature of the relationship change during the course of the poem?

B. Some critics of the *Iliad* have pointed out similarities between a god, Zeus, and the mortal, Akhilleus. Discuss what Zeus and Akhilleus are like. How are they similar and how are they different—in temperament? in their relations with peers? in how they influence the battle? in their attitudes toward the Trojans? Fill in the Venn diagram below.

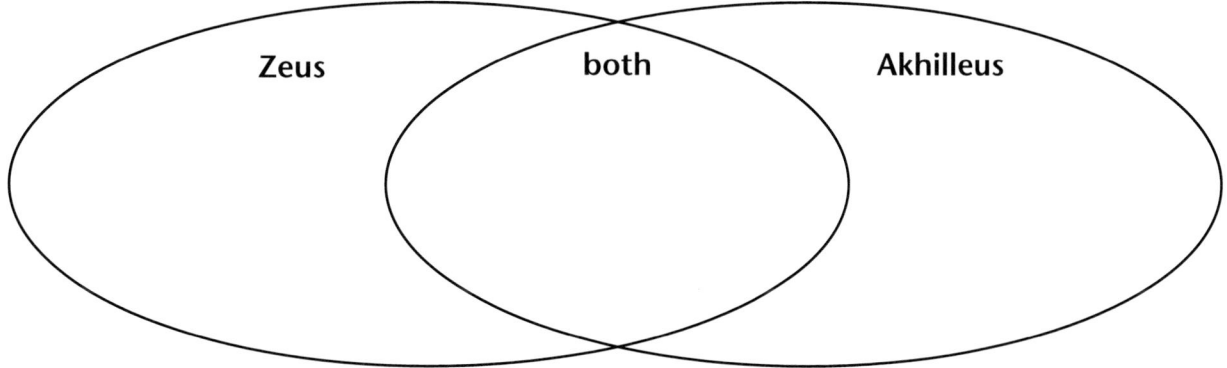

Write an essay beginning with the following topic sentence: "Zeus and Akhilleus mirror each other in interesting ways…" Use some of the following phrases to organize your thoughts: *also, likewise, in addition, on the whole, again, similarly, and yet…*

Name_____

The Iliad
Activity #9: Creative Writing
Use After Reading

Directions: The *Iliad* is full of great insults and gory descriptions. Here are a few:

Insults:
"Sack of wine, you with your cur's eyes and your antelope heart! You've never had the kidney to buckle on armor among the troops!"
"What a poltroon, how lily-livered I should be called if I..."
"...dog that he is..."
"...I would give not one dry shuck for him."
"milksop"
"The gall of him..."
"There that dogfly goes, bane of mankind..."

Gore:
"Through bronze and bone the spearhead broke into the brain within and left it spattered."
"...to cleave Pándaros' nose beside the eye and shatter his white teeth..."
"...but he brought his sword-blade in a flash down on the nape and severed the two tendons."

1. What is your favorite insult in the *Iliad*? (Cite Book and line.)

   _____

2. Who do you think meets the most gruesome end in the *Iliad*? (Cite Book and line.)

   _____

3. Pretend that you are a character in the *Iliad* and make up an insult worthy of Homer.

   I am (character): _____ I am insulting: _____

   Insult:

© Novel Units, Inc.   All rights reserved

Name_____

The Iliad
Activity #10: Satire
Use After Reading

Directions: Many of the characters and events in the *Iliad* have modern day counterparts in life, fiction, or art. For instance, you might see a similarity between the Greek and Trojan war, which started with tensions between Paris and Meneláos, and the 1995 government shutdown, which was fueled by tensions between Clinton and Gingrich. Or you might see a resemblance between the travails of "Father" Homer Simpson and Father Zeus. (If you're feeling creative, draw a cartoon that captures the *Iliad*-like nature of the present day situation.)

Iliad	Present Day Situation	Brief Explanation of the Similarity
conflict between Akhilleus and Agamémnon		
squabbling between Zeus and Hêra		
the war between Greeks and Trojans		
the killing of Dolôn		
the portent (serpent and hatchlings)		
Patróklos's ghost appearing to Akhilleus		
Hektor's treatment of Patróklos's body		
the angry river Xánthos		
the pleas of Hektor's parents		
the Greek wall		

Name_____

The Iliad
Activity #11: Critical Thinking
Use After Reading

Character Motivation

Directions: Lawrence Kohlberg evolved a model of moral development to explain what motivates an individual to act as he or she does. Kohlberg believes that his model can be applied to individuals of any culture. There are six levels of moral development in his model. All people do not reach the highest levels.

Decide which level best describes each character by the end of the poem.

Level I	Acts to avoid pain or punishment.	
Level II	Acts to get a reward.	
Level III	Acts to gain approval.	
Level IV	Acts because of belief in the law.	
Level V	Acts for the welfare of others.	
Level VI	Acts because of a self-formulated set of principles.	

Character	Level	Reason
Paris		
Agamémnon		
Akhilleus		
Odysseus		
Zeus		
Hêra		
Hektor		
Patróklos		
Nestor		
Helen		
Brisêis		
Diomédês		

© Novel Units, Inc.   All rights reserved

Name_____

The Iliad
Activity #12: Paraphrase/Homophones
Use After Reading

Directions: Homer's language isn't always easy for modern readers to follow. Students sometimes make mistakes when paraphrasing passages in the *Iliad*—often because a word used by Homer sounds like a word they know, but means something else. (If these words sound exactly alike but have different meanings, they are called **homophones**.) Below are several "bloopers" made by fictitious students. Replace each "blooper" with the correct statement or paraphrase.

Sample:
  a. Blooper: Troy took Helen to Paris.
  b. Correction: Paris took Helen to Troy.

1. a. Agamémnon told everyone who was thinking about dropping out of the fight against the Trojans to go fly a kite. (Book Two, line 462)
   b.

2. a. The Greeks made their envelopes out of bronze. (Book Three, line 299)
   b.

3. a. Nestor picked out a spear and dipped the tip in water. (Book Ten, line 149)
   b.

4. a. Paris said his mother didn't raise him to be a milkdud. (Book Thirteen, line 894)
   b.

5. a. Agamémnon swore he never hit Brisêis. (Book Nineteen, line 287)
   b.

6. a. The Trojan musicians cranked their hurdy-gurdies on the riverbanks. (Book Twenty-One, line 12)
   b.

7. a. The winner of the wrestling match got a camera tripod; the loser got a crafty woman. (Book Twenty-Three, lines 806-809)
   b.

8. a. Paris got mad and peeked at two goddesses. (Book Twenty-Four, line 33)
   b.

Name_____

The Iliad
Activity #13: Critical Thinking
Use After Reading

Directions: Several characters in the *Iliad* are faced with important decisions. Help them make these decisions by filling in decision-making grids like the one below for the problems listed. List all of the choices you can think of and criteria for measuring each choice. Then rate each choice by the "criteria" questions presented across the top of each chart. (1 = yes; 2 = no; 3 = maybe) Finally, choose one of the decisions and write an essay about the decision. (What was the decision? Why was it important? What choices did the character have? Did he make the best decision? Why or why not?)

Fill in this chart first. Then make similar charts for the other problems listed.

Problem: 1. How should Akhilleus respond to the three emissaries?

	Criteria:			
Possible Choices ↓	Will I save face?	Will I get revenge?	Will this anger any gods or goddesses?	Am I acting in a mature way?
Turn them away.				
Follow their advice.				
Tell them you'll think it over.				

Additional Problems: (Make a chart for each one.)
2. What should Agamémnon do after angering Akhilleus?
3. How should Dolôn respond to interrogation by Odysseus and Diomêdês?
4. How should Paris respond to disgruntled fellow Trojans?
5. How should Hektor respond to the pleas of his parents to save himself?

Name_____

The Iliad
Activity #14: Study Guide
Epic Style and Form

Directions: The *Iliad* is considered one of the most important folk epics. An **epic** is a long narrative poem in elevated style presenting heroic characters in a series of adventures.

This activity is designed to acquaint you with some of the characteristics and devices found in many epic poems: epic similes, catalogs, invocation of the muse, legendary heroes, vast setting, courageous action, supernatural forces, grand style, and epithets.

I. A simile is a comparison containing the words "like" or "as." Example: My hands are like ice. An Homeric simile is an **epic simile**, an unusually elaborate comparison that extends through a number of lines.
   Sample: "Aías/extending his broad shield above Patróklos, stood as a lion will above his cubs/when a hunting party comes upon the beast/in underbrush, leading his young." (Book Seventeen, lines 146-150)

A. For each simile below, read the lines noted and explain what two things are being compared—and how they are alike.
   1. "Being so dismissed, the Argives roared ... from any quarter rising" (Book Two, lines 463-467)

      _____ are like _____ because both

      _____.

   2. "As when a river in flood ... so Aías in his glory swept the field" (Book Eleven, lines 564-569)

      _____ is like _____ because both

      _____.

   3. "Artemis ran off in tears, as a wild dove ... where she cannot be taken." (Book Twenty-One, lines 573-576)

      _____ is like _____ because both

      _____.

Name_____

The Iliad
Study Guide—Epic Style and Form
page 2

Choose one of the following (B–E) and complete on separate paper or on the back of this sheet.

    B. Cite three other Homeric similes found in the Iliad. Put a star by your favorite one.

    C. Look for one of the longest similes you can find in the *Iliad* and cite the lines. Give a literal paraphrase of that passage, using as few words as possible.

    D. Share your simile and paraphrase with a partner.

    E. Compose your own Homeric simile to describe one of the following:
- a fight with your sibling
- a crowd you've been part of
- a time you ran away from something
- a frightening or lovely sound
- an inspiring view you recently saw
- something that caused you discomfort or pain

II. **Catalog.** A catalog is a listing of warriors, ships, armies, etc. Cite one example in the *Iliad*.

III. **Invocation of the muse.** Most epic poems open by stating the theme and invoking a Muse to inspire and instruct the poet. How does Homer invoke the Muse at the beginning of the *Iliad?* Cite the line numbers.

IV. *In media res.* Many epic poems begin "in the middle of the action." The *Iliad* begins in the midst of what conflict?

V. **Legendary heroes.** Epic poems contain legendary heroes engaged in courageous actions. Name three of the greatest heroes in the *Iliad*.

VI. **Setting.** The setting of most epic poems is grand in scope. What great nations figure in the *Iliad?*

VII. **Supernatural forces.** In most epic poems, there are supernatural forces such as gods, angels, and demons who interest themselves in the action and even step in from time into time. Provide three examples of this in the *Iliad*.

© Novel Units, Inc.   All rights reserved

Name_____

The Iliad
Study Guide—Epic Style and Form
page 3

VIII. Homeric Epithet: An adjectival phrase so often repeated in connection with a person or thing that it almost becomes a part of the name, as "great-lunged Meneláos." Homer used this repetition partly as an aid to remembering his lines.

A. Match each of the following epithets with the person or god/goddess it describes.

_____ 1. high commander, tamer of horses, lord marshall   a. Akhilleus
_____ 2. great runner, swift-footed   b. Zeus
_____ 3. white-armed goddess, wide-eyed ____   c. Apollo
_____ 4. grey-eyed goddess   d. Meneláos
_____ 5. gatherer of clouds, storm king, Father _____   e. Agamémnon
_____ 6. master mariner, tactician, wily commander, resourceful   f. Diomêdês
_____ 7. ____ of the silver bow, the bright archer   g. Aphrodítê
_____ 8. red-haired captain   h. Athêna
_____ 9. the rugged man, lord of the war cry   i. Iris
_____ 10. fierce war god   j. Hêra
_____ 11. wind-running ____   k. Hektor
_____ 12. the beautiful prince, master of horse   l. Dione
_____ 13. _____ of the shining helm, breaker of wild horses   m. Odysseus
_____ 14. pale-gold goddess   n. Arês
_____ 15. god who girdles earth   o. Patróklos
_____ 16. loveliest of goddesses   p. Poseidon
_____ 17. silvery-footed   q. Thetis

B. For each description, write the person or god/goddess it describes.

1. son of Atreus _____

2. son of Pêleus _____

3. son of Neleus _____

4. son of Krónos _____

5. daughter of Zeus _____

6. son of Laertes _____

Name_____

The Iliad
Study Guide—Epic Style and Form
page 4

7. father of Telemakhos _____

8. son of Lykaon _____

9. mother of Aineias, daughter of Zeus _____

10. son of Menoitios _____

11. son of Priam _____

12. brother of Hektor _____

13. daughter of Krónos _____

C. Create three newspaper headlines based on events in the *Iliad* that incorporate Homerian epithets. Sample: "Resourceful Odysseus Fails Diplomatic Mission"

1.

2.

3.

D. Try your hand at writing pithy epithets for each of the following:

the President   your best friend
the governor of your state   your employer
a current military dictator   your ideal self
a U.S. general   a political figure you admire
your favorite cartoon character   a political figure you dislike
a character on TV   your parent
your favorite athlete   your favorite teacher
your favorite actor

Name_____

The Iliad
Activity #15: Crossword Puzzle
(two pages: clues on page 26)

Crossword Challenge

Use the clues provided on the next page to fill in the correct answers to this crossword puzzle. You may find it helpful to use a book such as *The Greek Myths* by Robert Graves, *Bulfinch's Mythology*, or another book with information about Greek gods and goddesses.

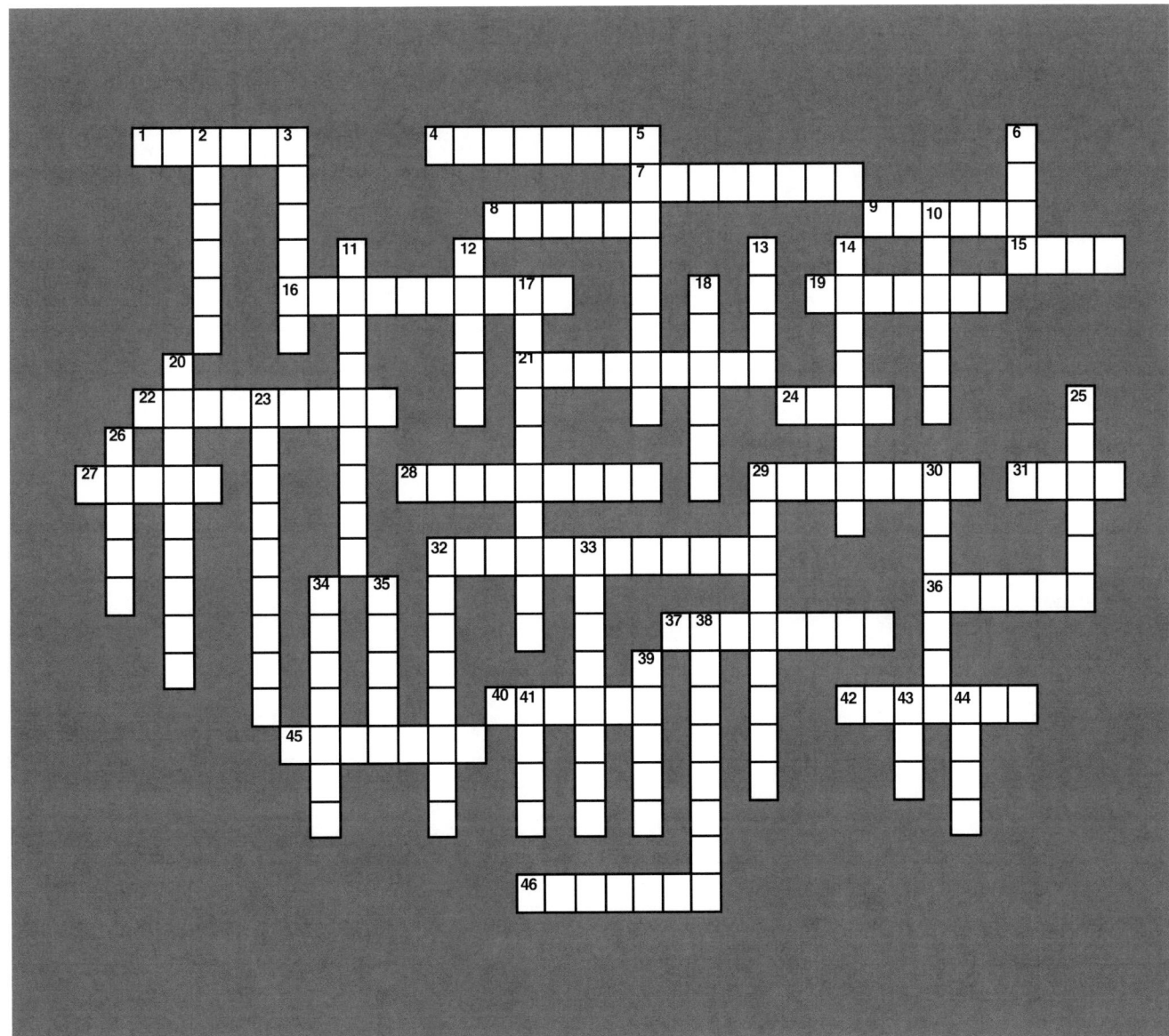

The Iliad
Activity #15: Crossword Puzzle
Clues

Name_____

Across

1. war-like grey-eyed goddess; daughter of Zeus
4. King of Argos, son of Tydeus
7. Greeks, along with Danáäns and Argives
8. son of Priam, chief warrior on the Trojan side
9. wisest and oldest Akhaian
15. AKA Ajax, son of Telmon
16. Trojan woman, wife of Hektor
19. vehicle behind which Akhilleus dragged Hektor's body
21. Akhilleus' best friend and counselor
22. river with which Akhilleus did battle
24. Homer began the *Iliad* with an invocation to the _____.
27. The *Iliad* begins *in* _____ *res.*
28. Akhilleus' tough army
29. Latinized version of "Akhilleus"
31. city also known as Ilion
32. wife of Agamémnon
36. sea nymph, mother of Akhilleus
37. god of the ocean, brother of Zeus
40. son of Zeus; made a plague arise
42. omen
45. mountain where the gods reside
46. chief seer of the Greeks

Down

2. wife of Priam
3. son of Aphrodítê and Anchises (Latinized spelling)
5. son of Zeus and Laodameia; King of Lycia
6. queen of the gods, sister and wife of Zeus
10. Hêphaistos made one for Akhilleus
11. ruler of Crete
12. His womanizing started trouble between the Greeks and Trojans.
13. king of the gods
14. daughter of a priest; abducted by Agamémnon
17. son of Hêra; lame blacksmith
18. father of Akhilleus
20. Agamémnon stirred his wrath and he refused to help the Greeks fight the Trojans.
23. goddess of love and beauty
25. father of Zeus
26. beautiful wife of Meneláos; union with Paris caused a lot of trouble
29. son of Atreus who angered Apollo by refusing to return the priest's daughter to her father
30. adjective phrase that almost becomes part of a name, e.g., "swift-footed Akhilleus"
32. shaped like horses, with human heads and torsos
33. King of Sparta, brother of Agamémnon
34. list of warriors, ships, armies, etc.
35. elderly King of Troy
38. King of Ithaca; good tactician
39. quick raid
41. pile of wood on which Hektor's body was burned
43. The *Iliad* begins *in media* _____.
44. long narrative poem in elevated style, e.g., the *Iliad, Beowulf*

Name_____

The Iliad
Comprehension Quiz • Books 1-12
Objective

Identification: (A) Label each of the following G (Greek) or T (Trojan).

____ 1. Agamémnon
____ 2. Meneláos
____ 3. Helen
____ 4. Priam
____ 5. Hekuba
____ 6. Sarpêdôn
____ 7. Akhilleus
____ 8. Patróklos
____ 9. Hektor
____ 10. Nestor
____ 11. Odysseus
____ 12. Paris
____ 13. Aías
____ 14. Diomêdês

(B) Label each of the follow GG (god/goddess allied with the Greeks) or GT (god/goddess allied with the Trojans).

____ 15. Aphrodítê
____ 16. Hêra
____ 17. Athêna
____ 18. Apollo
____ 19. Poseidon

True/False: Label each statement T (true) or F (false). (For bonus points, rewrite false statements on the back of the paper to make them true.)

____ 20. Agamémnon is angry with Akhilleus because Agamémnon kidnapped Akhilleus's child.
____ 21. Zeus sends Agamémnon a false dream to make him think that Troy is about to fall to the Greeks.
____ 22. Paris ran off with Meneláos's wife, Helen.
____ 23. Zeus's wife Hêra wants the Trojans to win.
____ 24. Apollo, Aphrodítê, and Árês are on the side of the Trojans.
____ 25. Diomêdês and Glaukos decide not to fight because their grandfathers swore to be friends.
____ 26. The Trojans offer to give the Greeks some treasure back, but they decline.
____ 27. Zeus predicts that Akhilleus will join the fray after his father, Hektor, is killed.
____ 28. Phoenix, Odysseus, and Aías approach Akhilleus and ask him to stay out of the war.
____ 29. Diomêdês and Odysseus get information from Dolôn, then spare his life when he begs for mercy.
____ 30. Akhilleus sends Patróklos to Nestor to ask about the wounded man Nestor is tending.
____ 31. Led by Hektor, the Trojans reach the Greek fortifications.

Name_____

The Iliad
Comprehension Quiz • Level I
page 2

Matching: Match each cause with its effect

Causes

___ 32. Apollo's anger at Agamémnon

___ 33. Agamémnon's dream

___ 34. Paris brings home a married woman.

___ 35. Pándaros shoots Meneláos.

___ 36. Aphrodítê tries to save her mortal son.

___ 37. Hektor asks his mother to petition Athêna to keep Diomêdês out of Troy.

___ 38. Trojans ask Paris to give Helen back to the Greeks.

___ 39. Zeus forbids the gods to fight.

___ 40. Akhilleus is still angry with Agamémnon.

___ 41. Dolôn tells Odysseus and Diomêdês that the Thracians have arrived.

___ 42. Eurypylos asks for a hand.

___ 43. An eagle drops a snake among the Trojans.

Effects

A. Trojans go to war with the Greeks.

B. Greeks are tricked into preparing for battle without Akhilleus.

C. The emissaries fail to get his help in saving the Akhaian army.

D. Plague on the Greeks

E. Poulydamas advises Hektor not to push forward against the Greeks.

F. The Trojan women visit a shrine.

G. Truce between Greeks and Trojans is broken.

H. Patróklos helps clean a wound.

I. Two Greeks kill a king and acquire lovely horses.

J. Prince Alexandros refuses.

K. The Greeks are hard pressed without the help of Hêra and Athêna.

L. Diomêdês wounds a goddess.

Name_____

The Iliad
Comprehension Quiz • Books 1-12
Short Essay

Directions: Several incidents which appear in the first 12 books of the *Iliad* are listed below. Choose 10 of these, and describe **each one** in one short paragraph. (Use separate paper.)

1. Agamémnon ignites the wrath of Akhilleus.
2. Zeus sends Agamémnon a false dream.
3. Paris and Meneláos engage in a contest.
4. A bowshot ends the truce.
5. Diomêdês wounds two gods.
6. Diomêdês and Glaukos decide not to fight.
7. The Trojans make the Greeks an offer.
8. Zeus sways a battle and makes a prediction.
9. Three emissaries pay a call.
10. Two Greeks go on a night reconnaissance patrol.
11. Hektor joins the fray and Akhilleus thinks about it.
12. The rampart is breached.

Name_____

The Iliad
Unit Test • Objective
page 1

Identification: Find the description on the right that matches the character on the left. Write the letter of the description next to the matching number.

____ 1. Akhilleus

____ 2. Agamémnon

____ 3. Helen

____ 4. Brisêis

____ 5. Zeus

____ 6. Hêra

____ 7. Hektor

____ 8. Odysseus

____ 9. Paris

____ 10. Meneláos

____ 11. Priam

____ 12. Patróklos

____ 13. Apollo

____ 14. Diomêdês

____ 15. Thetis

A. Mother of Akhilleus; obtained a shield for him
B. AKA Alexandros: Trojan abductor of Helen
C. Akhilleus wept when he gave up this woman, his "prize."
D. King of Ithaca; patient and practical
E. The high commander who demanded to have Akhilleus's "girl"
F. His anger at Agamémnon kept him from helping the Akhaians.
G. Elderly king of Troy, father of Hektor and Paris
H. Ruler of the gods
I. Greek king of Argos; son of Tydeus
J. Akhilleus's companion; Thetis kept his body whole
K. A war was ignited when Paris took this beautiful wife of Meneláos.
L. God of archery; allied with Trojans
M. Greek king; husband of Helen, brother of Agamémnon
N. Leader of the Trojan forces
O. Sister and consort of Zeus, allied with the Greeks

Multiple Choice: Choose the **best** answer.

____ 16. Poseidon disobeyed Zeus by
   A. making a shield for Akhilleus.
   B. helping the Trojans build a wall.
   C. rallying the Greeks to fight.
   D. dropping a snake on the Greeks.

Name_____

The Iliad
Unit Test • Objective
page 2

___ 17. As a result of Hêra's trickery, Zeus
    A. fell asleep
    B. killed Apollo
    C. lost his talking horses
    D. married Aphrodítê

___ 18. Led by Apollo, the Trojans reached the Greek ships and
    A. sank them with lead ingots
    B. set fire to them
    C. sailed away on them
    D. removed the gold from them

___ 19. Patróklos persuaded Akhilleus to let him
    A. duel with Paris
    B. duel with Agamémnon
    C. give his armor to Hektor
    D. lead the Myrmidons in battle

___ 20. Hektor fought the Greeks for Patróklos's body because he wanted to
    A. defile and ruin it
    B. use it as ransom for Sarpêdôn's body
    C. give his friend a decent funeral
    D. strip the helmet from it

___ 21. Thetis went to Hêphaistos and asked him to make a new _____ for Akhilleus.
    A. chariot
    B. shield
    C. harp
    D. set of boots

___ 22. On the fourth day of battle Agamémnon offered gifts to Akhilleus and
    A. presented him with a pet boar
    B. had a door slammed in his face
    C. was reconciled with him
    D. sacrificed Brisêis to the gods

23. The following gods were allied with the Trojans
    A. Hêra, Athêna, Poseidon
    B. Hêra, Athêna, Apollo
    C. Aphrodítê, Apollo, Arês
    D. Zeus, Hades, Hêphaistos

24. After driving Trojans into the water, Akhilleus was nearly drowned by the angry river _____
    A. Ilion
    B. Xánthos
    C. Argos
    D. Pylos

25. Hektor was killed by
    A. Athêna
    B. Agamémnon
    C. Diomêdês
    D. Akhilleus

26. Akhilleus was reconciled with the Greeks and presided over funeral games in honor of
    A. Hektor
    B. Patróklos
    C. Diomêdês
    D. Sarpêdôn

27. Priam called on Akhilleus and asked him for
    A. Hektor's body
    B. Sarpêdôn's body
    C. Brisêis
    D. Helen

Name_____

The Iliad
Unit Test • Objective
page 4

Fill-Ins: Fill in each blank with a word from the list.

Danáäns	shield	sortie	wife	food	Trojans
chariot	anodyne	wrath	gold	pyre	portent
mother	carrion	shade			

28. Homer uses three terms to describe Greeks (living in different communities). These are Akhaians, Argives, and _____.

29. The Greeks were rallied by Poseidon, but Hektor and the _____ still came on.

30. _____ was sprinkled on a warrior's wound to heal it and relieve the pain.

31. Akhilleus was worried that while he fought, black _____ flies would settle on Patróklos's body.

32. Priam and Hekuba begged Hektor to think of his _____ Andromakhe, and come inside to safety.

33. Akhilleus's _____ Thetis told him the gods were angry and wanted the body of Hektor released.

34. The serpent's eating nine birds was considered a _____ that the Greeks would wage war for nine years and take Troy on the tenth.

35. The bodies of Greek and Trojan heroes were burned on a funeral _____.

36. Patróklos's ghost, or _____, appeared to Akhilleus and begged him to see that his body was given proper rites.

37. Odysseus suggested that before going into the decisive battle, the soldiers should be given _____.

© Novel Units, Inc.   All rights reserved

Name_____

The Iliad
Unit Test • Essay/Short Essay
page 1

Short Answer: Write your answers in complete sentences.

1. Whose side was Poseidon on? Why was he so enraged by Hektor's killing Amphimakhos?

2. How did Hêra trick Zeus—and why?

3. Which god led the Trojans in their advance to the Greek ships—and what did they do when they reached the ships?

4. What did Akhilleus lend Patróklos—and why?

5. How did Patróklos die, and what happened to his body?

6. Who visited lame Hêphaistos—and why?

7. How were Akhilleus and Agamémnon reconciled? What are some of the gifts Agamémnon gave, and what was the promise he made?

8. How did Hektor escape from Akhilleus and what was Akhilleus's response?

9. Who did battle with the river Skamander—and why?

10. How did Athêna trick Hektor into fighting Akhilleus in Hektor's final battle?

11. What did Patróklos's ghost ask—and whose death did he predict?

12. What finally happened to Hektor's body?

Name_____

The Iliad
Unit Test • Essay/Short Essay
page 2

13-15. Homeric Hero Award: Pretend that you are presenting an award to your favorite Homeric hero. Fill in the following chart with the hero's name and three reasons he should get the award.

```
Name: _____

1. Heroism in Battle: _____

2. _____

3. _____
```

16-18. Theme:
The themes of compassion and solidarity are developed throughout the *Iliad*—especially the final book. In each box, below, briefly explain how the situation is a demonstration of compassion/solidarity.

Akhilleus' treatment of Hektor's body

Akhilleus' treatment of Priam

Prince Hektor's funeral

Name_____

The Iliad
Unit Test •Essay/Short Essay
page 3

Quote Identification: Identify the speaker in each case and put his/her statement into your own words.

19. "You bad-luck charm! Paris, the great lover, a gallant sight!/ You should have had no seed and died unmarried./ Would to god you had!/ Better than living this way in dishonor,/ in everyone's contempt"

20. "No need to sit with me like mourning doves/making your gentle noise by turns. I hate/ as I hate Hell's own gate that man who hides one thought within him while he speaks another./ What I shall say is what I see and think. Give in to Agamémnon? I think not."

21. "But I am not to blame./ Zeus and Fate and a nightmare Fury are,/ for putting savage Folly in my mind/ in the assembly that day, when I wrested/ Akhilleus' prize of war from him. Divine will shapes these things./ Ruinous Folly, eldest daughter of Zeus,/ beguiles us all."

22. "Sleeping so? Thou has forgotten me,/ Akhilleus. Never was I uncared for/ in life but am in death. Accord me burial/ in all haste."

23. "O immortal madness, why do you have this craving to seduce me? Am I to be transported even farther eastward, into some Phyrgian walled town/ or into Meionie, if you have there another mortal friend? Is it because Meneláos has beaten Alexandros and, hateful though I am, would take me home?"

Name_____

The Iliad
Unit Test • Essay/Short Essay
page 4

24. **Essay:** (Choose three.) Each essay should include at least three examples or reasons taken directly from the *Iliad* as supportive evidence.

   1. Describe similarities between Zeus and Akhilleus.
   2. Explain how Akhilleus changes—and why.
   3. Write a character sketch of your favorite character in the *Iliad*.
   4. Trace how one of the following themes is developed in the *Iliad*:
      - "women as property"
      - gift-giving and supplication
      - vengeance vs. compassion
      - saving face
      - manliness and loyalty
   5. Support or refute one of the the following statements, using evidence from the *Iliad*.
      - Homer's gods display all too human weaknesses.
      - Homer's gods constantly intervene in the action, reducing the heroes to mere pawns.
      - Homer's gods lighten the tone of the *Iliad,* providing moments of comedy.

25. **Creative Thinking and Writing:** (Choose three.) Let your imaginations fly—but include details from the story.

   1. Write an obituary for one of the fallen heroes who dies in the course of the *Iliad*.
   2. You are Hektor. Write a letter home to your wife.
   3. You are Meneláos. Write the Valentine note you never had the chance to give Helen.
   4. You are Agamémnon. Write your thoughts as you listen to Agamémnon propose that you forget your differences.
   5. You are Akhilleus. Write down the dream you have the night you learn that your best friend is dead.

Answer Key

Activities #1 and #2: are open-ended activities with no right/wrong answers. Students should be given time to discuss their answers with partners, in small groups, or as a class.

Study Questions
Book One
1. Homer asks the muse to tell the story of how Akhilleus's anger resulted in death and destruction for the Greeks.
2. Apollo punished the Greeks with a plague when Agamémnon refused to return a daughter to her father, the priest Khryses.
3. Agamémnon took the "girl," Brisêis, from Akhilleus.
4. Akhilleus originally came to help Agamémnon get revenge on the Trojans for something they did to Agamémnon's brother, but Akhilleus was angry about losing Brisêis and withdrew from battle.
5. Acting on her son Akhilleus's request, Thetis asked Zeus to take the Trojan side until Agamémnon and the Akhaians repay her son.
6. Jealous Hêra had demanded to know what Thetis wanted.

Book Two
1. Zeus sent Agamémnon a dream that convinced the leader Troy was about to fall to the Greeks.
2. Agamémnon, tricked into preparing for battle, tested his troops' loyalty by telling them to go home. They stayed only when Nestor and Odysseus reasoned with them.
3. Nestor thought this would foster loyalty and help determine which men were cowards.

Book Three
1. If Paris killed Meneláos, he could keep Helen and the gold. If Paris were killed, the Trojans would surrender Helen and the treasure.
2. She made him disappear from the contest and took him to his bedroom.
3. Lines 518-519: "Home from the war?/ You should have perished there,/ brought down by that strong soldier, once my husband."
4. The Greeks claimed victory by default since Paris had disappeared.

Book Four
1. Hêra, who sided with the Greeks, didn't like Zeus's suggestion that Troy should be spared and the war should end now with Helen going back to Meneláos.
2. Athêna disguised herself as a Trojan soldier and egged on Pándaros, a Trojan archer, so that he would shoot Meneláos.
3. His injury was minor but the truce was broken.

Book Five
1. Diomêdês killed Pándaros.
2. Athêna and Hêra sided with the Greeks.
3. Apollo, Aphrodítê, and Arês sided with the Trojans.
4. Aphrodítê and Arês returned to Olympus after being wounded by Diomêdês.

Book Six
1. Hektor was the brother of Paris/Alexandros.
2. Hektor wanted Athêna to rein in Diomêdês so that he would cease his slaughter of the Trojans.
3. Diomêdês and Glaukos discovered that their grandfathers had sworn friendship.
4. Hektor's baby began to wail at the sight of his helmet.

Book Seven
1. Neither Hektor nor Aías won.
2. The truce was called so that burials could be done.
3. Lines 411-415: "Trojans, Dardans and allies...Bring Argive Helen...and let us give her back to the Atreidai..."
4. The Greeks refused the Trojans' offer to give up the treasure that Paris had brought to Troy with Helen.

Book Eight
1. Zeus ordered the gods to stay out of the mortals' fight.
2. Hektor led the Trojans.
3. Akhilleus would join the fray after the death of his friend, Patróklos.
4. Lines 637-640: "There were a thousand burning in the plain..."

Book Nine
1. Diomêdês spoke against Agamémnon, reminding them they had responsibilities.
2. The three emissaries were Odysseus, Phoenix, and Aías.
3. They appealed to Akhilleus to help the Greeks fight the Trojans.
4. Akhilleus vowed that he wouldn't join the fight no matter what, and that he was thinking about sailing for home in the morning.

Book Ten
1. Diomêdês agreed to go on a reconnaissance patrol behind Trojan lines.
2. Odysseus was considered a good tactician, practical and patient.
3. They let him believe that they would spare his life if he gave them information about the Trojans, then killed him.
4. They killed King Rhêsos and many Thracians, then took their lovely horses.

Book Eleven
1. Diomêdês, Odysseus, Makhaon, and Agamémnon were all wounded.
2. Hektor was to stay out of battle until Agamémnon was hurt.
3. Akhilleus wanted Patróklos to find out about the wounded man Nestor was tending.
4. Nestor suggested that Patróklos advise Akhilleus to let him (Patróklos) lead the Myrmidons into battle against the Trojans.
5. When Eurypylos was wounded, Patróklos tended his wounds.

Book Twelve
1. Hektor led the attack.
2. Poulydamas suggested that the Trojans should cross the moat on foot.
3. Poulydamas suggested that Hektor should pay attention to the portent—and lead the Trojans on a retreat.
4. Sarpêdôn charged the wall with his cousin, Glaukos.

Book Thirteen
1. The god, Poseidon, defied Zeus and helped the Greeks.
2. The Greeks made their stand around the two Aías.
3. Paris vowed that he would show courage in battle.
4. Zeus planned to give the Trojans a limited victory.

Book Fourteen
1. Diomêdês, Odysseus, and Agamémnon were all wounded.
2. Odysseus thought the plan cowardly.
3. Hêra put Zeus to sleep so that Poseidon would have a chance to help the Greeks.
4. Hektor was carried off after being wounded by a stone.

Book Fifteen
1. Furious Zeus ordered Poseidon to withdraw from the battle.
2. Zeus predicted that Akhilleus would send Patróklos into battle, Hektor would kill Patróklos, Akhilleus would kill Hektor, the Greeks would take Troy.
3. Apollo led the Trojans.
4. Patróklos wanted to convince Akhilleus to come to the aid of the Greeks.

Book Sixteen
1. Akhilleus let Patróklos lead the Myrmidons in battle.
2. Akhilleus gave Patróklos his armor.
3. Apollo, Euphórbus, and Hektor joined in killing Patróklos.
4. Patróklos predicted Hektor's death at Akhilleus's hands.

Book Seventeen
1. Hektor took the armor Akhilleus had given Patróklos.
2. Glaukos wanted to trade the body for that of Glaukos's cousin, Sarpêdôn.
3. Hektor wanted to defile the body, but the Greeks retrieved it.
4. The runner was sent to tell Akhilleus of Patróklos's death.

Book Eighteen
1. Akhilleus was grief-stricken about Patróklos's death.
2. Thetis predicted the death of her son, Akhilleus, soon after Hektor's.
3. Akhilleus vowed to kill twelve Trojans.
4. Thetis asked the lame blacksmith to make new armor for Akhilleus.

Book Nineteen
1. Thetis promised to keep Patróklos's body from decaying and advised her son to reconcile with Agamémnon.
2. Odysseus advised Akhilleus to feed the men before battle.
3. Agamémnon gave Akhilleus gold, women, horses—and a promise that he hadn't touched Brisêis.
4. He had already accepted his fate, but wouldn't die without a fight.

Book Twenty
1. Greeks: Hêra, Athêna, Poseidon, Hermês, Hêphaistos. Trojans: Arês, Phoibus, Apollo, Artemis, Leto, Xánthos, Aphrodîte
2. Poseidon helped this Trojan—even though usually on the side of the Greeks—because Aíneias was destined to rule over the Trojan survivors.
3. Apollo helped protect Hektor by hiding him in a cloud.
4. No, Akhilleus stabbed Trôs as Trôs begged for mercy.

Book Twenty-One
1. He had disturbed and polluted the clean, peaceful waters.
2. Athêna fought with Arês and Aphrodítê, Hêra fought with Artemis.
3. As Agênor faced Akhilleus, Apollo whisked Agênor away and hid him in the mist.
4. Apollo pretended to be Agênor to lure Akhilleus away while the Trojans reached safety in the walled town.

Book Twenty-Two
1. Hektor was stranded outside, where he stood fast to fight Akhilleus.
2. They begged him not to fight Akhilleus alone, to think of how they and his wife and child would grieve his loss. Hektor felt he must stay to save face.
3. Athêna pretended to be Hektor's brother and told them they would stand together and take Akhilleus on.
4. After killing Hektor, Akhilleus dragged the body behind his chariot.

Book Twenty-Three
1. Patróklos's "shade" requested a speedy burial.
2. Akhilleus ordered his Myrmidons to ride their chariots ahead, and infantry to follow the body. He cut his hair and offered sheep as a sacrifice, sheathed the body in fat, threw horses, dogs, and the bodies of 12 Trojans on the fire, poured libations to the winds, then consigned the body of Patróklos to the flames.
3. The bones were packed in a golden urn with sheepfat until a tomb could be built.
4. The funeral games included wrestling, chariot-racing, running, archery, spear-throwing, discus-tossing.

Book Twenty-Four
1. Iris was sent to convince Akhilleus's mother to persuade him to give up Hektor's body. Iris went to Priam to tell him to prepare gifts and go to Akhilleus to petition for Hektor's body.
2. When Thetis told her son that the gods were angry with him for keeping Hektor's body, he didn't argue with her—but told her to let someone bring the ransom and take the dead away.
3. Priam was all for going, while his wife urged him to stay with her and not risk his life.
4. Akhilleus gave up Hektor's body and the poem ends with a description of Hektor's funeral.

Activity #3: 1-B; 2-E; 3-D; 4-G; 5-A; 6-I; 7-F; 8-J; 9-H; 10-C

Activity #4: 1-Menelános; 2-Paris; 3-Agamémnon; 4-Khrysêis; 5-Brisêis; 6-Akhilleus; 7-Zeus; 8-Hêra; 9-Aphrodítê; 10-Apollo

Activities #5, #6 and #7: Personal response

Activity #8: Agamémnon is Akhilleus's military leader; there is great animosity between the two; Akhilleus feels exploited by Agamémnon and considers him self-serving. Zeus has affection for Hêra but gets annoyed by her readiness to challenge him; she is angry with him for the help he gives the Trojans

Activities #9, #10 and #11: Individual response

Activity #12:
1b- Agamémnon threatened deserters that they would end up as a meal for hawks.
2b- The Greeks were wearing bronze armor.
3b- He picked a spear tipped with sharpened bronze.
4b- Paris said his mother didn't raise him to be a coward (milksop).
5b- Agamémnon swore he had never slept with Brisêis.
6b- The Trojans made a commotion as they plunged into the river.

7b- The winner got a three-armed metal device for cooking over the fire; the loser got a woman skilled at crafts.

8b- Paris made a crazy decision and angered two goddesses.

Activity #13: Personal response

Activity #14: I. 1. The Argives are like the stormy sea hitting a rock; both roar. 2. Aías is like a swollen river that scatters trees; both sweep away bodies. 3. Artemis is like a dove that has been attacked; both fly away to safety. B-E: Answers will vary.

II. Sample: Book Two—listing of Greek and Trojan armies
III. Homer begins by asking the Muse to tell the "song" of Akhilleus's anger. (Line numbers 1-10)
IV. Agamémnon has created a problem by refusing to return Khrysêis to her father.
V. Sample: Akhilleus (G); Hektor (T); Diomêdês (G)
VI. The Greek nations (e.g., Mycenae; Lacedaemon; Phthia, etc.) and Troy
VII. the gods and goddesses; the talking horses; Patróklos's ghost
VIII. **A.** 1-E; 2-A; 3-J; 4-H; 5-B; 6-M; 7-C; 8-D; 9-F; 10-N; 11-I; 12-O; 13-K; 14-G; 15-P; 16-L; 17-Q
B. 1-Agamémnon; 2-Akhilleus; 3-Nestor; 4-Zeus; 5-Athêna; 6-Odysseus; 7-Odysseus; 8-Pándaros; 9-Aphrodítê; 10-Patróklos; 11-Hektor; 12-Paris; 13-Hêra
C and D: Personal response

Activity #15: Crossword Puzzle

Comprehension Quiz, Objective
I. Identification: A: 1-G; 2-G; 3-G; 4-T; 5-T; 6-T; 7-G; 8-G; 9-T; 10-G; 11-G; 12-T; 13-G; 14-G;
B: 15-GT; 16-GG; 17-GG; 18-GT; 19-GT
II. True/False: 20-F; 21-T; 22-T; 23-F; 24-T; 25-T; 26-T; 27-F; 28-F; 29-F; 30-T; 31-T
III. Cause-Effect: 32-D; 33-B; 34-A; 35-G; 36-L; 37-F; 38-J; 39-K; 40-C; 41-I; 42-H; 43-E

Comprehension Quiz, Short Essay
These summaries will vary. See the synopses of Books One–Twelve found in the teaching guide for key points that the summaries should cover.

Unit Test, Objective
Identification: 1-F; 2-E; 3-K; 4-C; 5-H; 6-O; 7-N; 8-D; 9-B; 10-M; 11-G; 12-J; 13-L; 14-I; 15-A
Multiple Choice: 16-C; 17-A; 18-B; 19-D; 20-A; 21-B; 22-C; 23-C; 24-B; 25-D; 26-B; 27-A
Fill-Ins: 28-Danääns; 29-Trojans; 30-Anodyne; 31-carrion; 32-wife; 33-mother; 34-portent; 35-pyre; 36-shade; 37-food
Suggested Scoring: 3 points each for 1-27; 2 points each for 28-37

Unit Test, Essay/Short Essay
Short Answer:
1. Poseidon was on the side of the Greeks and was enraged by Hektor's killing his grandson.
2. Hêra seduced Zeus so that he would sleep while Poseidon aided the Greeks in battle.
3. Apollo led the Trojans in their advance on the Greek ships, which they burned.
4. Akhilleus gave Patróklos his armor so that Patróklos would stay safe as he led the Myrmidons in battle.
5. Apollo, Euphorbus and Hektor ganged up on him and killed him when he failed to heed Akhilleus's warning not to go too far. His body was rescued by the Greeks.
6. Thetis visited the lame blacksmith to ask him to make a new shield for her son, Akhilleus, because Hektor had taken the shield from Patróklos's body.
7. Thetis advised her son to call the Akhaians and tell them his anger with Agamémnon was done with. Agamémnon sacrificed a boar, produced women, gold, horses and promised that he had not laid a finger on Brisêis.
8. Apollo protected Hektor by hiding him in a cloud and Akhilleus, enraged, slayed many Trojans.
9. Akhilleus did battle with the river, whose god was angered by Akhilleus's driving Trojans into his waters and polluting them.
10. Athêna pretended to be Hektor's brother and told him they would stand together against Akhilleus.
11. Patróklos asked Akhilleus to see that he was given a speedy, proper burial—and predicted Akhilleus's death.
12. After Priam visited Akhilleus, Akhilleus finally gave up Hektor's body to the Trojans and it was given proper funeral rites (burned on a pyre).

13-15. **Homeric Hero Award:** Answers will vary. (Make sure the student has provided three examples of the hero's courage.)

16-18. **Theme:** Answers will vary. Students should point out that Akhilleus showed no compassion at first by dragging the body around—then treated Priam kindly and gave the body back so that the Trojan people could hold the funeral and begin to heal. Akhilleus put aside his personal grievance for the "better good" of the Greeks as a whole; the gods had made it clear that they didn't like his withholding the body—and Hektor knew they might punish Akhilleus's people if he persisted. Akhilleus agreed to a "cease-fire" for twelve days following Hektor's funeral, so proper rites could be performed and time for mourning allowed.

Quote Identification:
19. Hektor: You are bad news, brother Paris. Everyone hates you. It would have been better if you had died before abducting Helen.
20. Akhilleus: Emissaries, you don't have to try to be diplomatic. I'll tell it like it is: I'm still mad at Agamémnon and I'm not about to give in and help in the battle.
21. Agamémnon: Akhilleus, I regret what happened but it was Fate—not my fault. I couldn't help myself when I took Akhilleus's woman from him.
22. Patróklos's ghost: Akhilleus, how can you forget about me? See to my proper burial!
23. Helen: Aphrodítê, why are you trying to get me together with Paris? Are you afraid that my first husband Meneláos is going to take me back?

24. **Essay:** Answers will vary, but students who answer #1 or #2 should include the following key points.
1. Akhilleus and Agamémnon's argument is similar to Zeus and Hêra's. Both Akhilleus and Zeus are isolated from their peers; both watch intensely as the Trojans burn the Greek ships.
2. Akhilleus softens, overcomes his personal anger against Agamémnon for the good of the Greeks as a whole.

25. **Creative Thinking and Writing:** Answers will vary.

Suggested Scoring for Unit Test: 1-12: 2 points each (total 24); 13-23: 3 points each (total 33); 9 points each for essay (total 27); 5 for each creative writing (total 15)